This book is dedicated to all who find Nature not an adversary to conquer and destroy, but a storehouse of infinite knowledge and experience linking man to all things past and present. They know conserving the natural environment is essential to our future well-being.

D1537288

GREAT SMOKY MOUNTAINS

THE STORY BEHIND THE SCENERY®

by W. Eugene Cox

W. Eugene Cox, is the former Chief of Interpretation and Visitor Services at Great Smoky Mountains National Park. His career has been dedicated to conservation and education and to providing the best possible service for the park's most important resource, the visitor.

Great Smoky Mountains National Park, *located in Tennessee and North Carolina, was established in 1934 to preserve the rich biological and cultural diversity in this wildlands sanctuary.*

Front cover: Shot Beech Ridge and Deep Creek Valley, photo by George Humphries. Inside front cover: Catawba rhododendrons, photo by Pat O'Hara. Page 1: River otter, photo by Bill Lea. Pages 2/3: Middle Prong of the Little Pigeon River, photo by George Humphries.

Edited by Cheri C. Madison. Book design by K. C. DenDooven.

Ninth Printing • 2005 • New Version

N Named for the extinct passenger pigeon,
the middle prong of the Little Pigeon River

reminds us of the creation of these ancient mountains and just how fragile plant and animal life is.

JEFF GNASS

Great Smoky Mountains
National Park contains more
than 50 peaks over 5,000
feet in elevation, with 16 of
these exceeding 6,000 feet.
The diverse and complex
ecosystem covers just over
a half million acres. Water
created the diversity of life,
with 80 inches of precipitaion
occurring at Clingmans
Dome and 54 inches at
Gatlinburg. The Great
Smoky Mountains provide
the only habitat in the world
for many plant and animal
species, and the park
contains one of the largest
remaining virgin forests
of the great wilderness which
once covered eastern America.
It is the most visited national
park in America. The unique
and different forests provide
the most beautiful colors
found anywhere, and during
the full color season there
is no better place to be than
in the Great Smoky Mountains.

*John and Lucretia Oliver built
their second home in the early
1820s near a spring that would
be their water suppply.*

The Great Smoky Mountains Story

ADAM JONES

The Great Smoky Mountains story is a blending of geology showing one of the oldest mountain ranges in North America, with Indian culture and the settling of the Europeans into the Appalachian chain. Rocks alone don't tell the story --- people, and the living flora and fauna weave together a tale of America and it's cultural roots.

Along the pathways we witness the now silent forces of mountain building, erosion and the effects of vegetation that helped form these peaks and valleys. The Park is habitat to such a diversity of life that there is now a major campaign underway just to identify all the elements of plants, trees, animals, birds, insects - and all the things that call Great Smoky Mountains National Park, home.

The ancestors of the Cherokees came to the Smoky Mountains to establish it as their homeland. About 500 years ago the first Europeans arrived. In the 1800s settlers moved on to the land. Open flat areas like Cades Cove show us today how life was in the early days. We can now visit sites that show how people went about their daily life - from birth to death.

As with many of our Park areas, there came a time to see the wisdom of setting land and its elements aside for future generations to enjoy, and appreciate. Because of the foresight of leaders in the late 1800s and early 1900s, the land we see today was designated as a National Park in 1934.

Today we come to understand and appreciate what our forefathers understood. The Great Smoky Mountains National Park is one of the few parks that straddles two states. Both Tennessee and North Carolina revel in

Many trees in the Albright Grove—named for Horace M. Albright, second Director of the National Park Service—were fortunate to have escaped the logger's saw when this area was selectively cut over. This tuliptree is 22 feet 9 inches in circumference. In the 1930s one tuliptree along the Thunderhead Prong was named "Black Bill Walker's Walking Stick." It measured 25 feet in circumference.

Charlies Bunion, a popular destination for hikers, offers a spectacular view for those who make the eight-mile round trip. Wildflowers are plentiful along the trail. In 1925, 600-million-year-old rocks were exposed when the area was denuded of vegetation by a fire.

PAT & CHUCK BLACKLEY

having this scenic wonder in "their" state. The road through the Park serves both as an introduction of what is beyond the overlooks, as well as an important route of commerce between the two states.

Each fall the myriad of colors nature provides is a constant source of beauty. How beautiful a single leaf can be. It's nature's way of signaling the end of summer and the approaching winter season.

We didn't create the scenery we enjoy. We created the boundary to say where it is, and gave it a name: Great Smoky Mountains National Park. Come see and enjoy.

One of the most visited sites in the park, the John P. Cable water-powered grist mill still grinds corn on its original site. The wooden millrace is 235 feet long. Built in the early 1870s, the mill was restored by the Civilian Conservation Corps in 1935-36 for just under $3,000.

SALVATORE VASAPOLLI

*The Smoky Mountains are part of
the ancient Appalachian mountain chain
that runs southwest to northeast,
a distance of about 2,000 miles,
from central Alabama to Newfoundland.*

The Shaping of Life

GENE COX

One of my first memories of Great Smoky Mountains National Park is seeing fog slowly rise up the mountainside like smoke from a hidden campfire. An almost ghostlike mist was swirling among the branches where cool and warm air mix. Perhaps Native Americans were thinking the same when they named these mountains *shaconage*—place of blue smoke.

OLD ROCKS AND LANDSCAPES

The Cherokee Indians who live adjacent to the park have a legend that tells of the forming of these mountains. In the beginning all living things lived in the sky. When the "sky vault" that they called home became too crowded with people and animals, the People began to ask what was below the ocean which could be seen from their home. To find out, the People sent a little water beetle down to look for land in the ocean.

When the beetle could find no place to rest, it dived to the bottom and brought up some mud, which grew to form the earth. While the land was soft, flat, and wet, a buzzard was sent down to find a place to live. After searching for a long time, the buzzard became very tired and, sinking low, his

In what seems to be an impossible growing situation, *this lone Fraser fir is established on Thunderhead sandstone. This sandstone ranges from 6,000 to 12,000 feet thick. It makes up much of the north-facing slope from Mount Le Conte to Mount Cammerer, and waterfalls such as Ramsay Cascades and Rainbow Falls flow across it.*

NYE SIMMONS

*B*arren, windswept rocks *frame the dawn panorama of Greenbrier Pinnacle, Mount Guyot, and Laurel Top. Ridge upon ridge can be seen from Myrtle Point on Mount Le Conte, the third highest mountain in the park. A concession-operated lodge on Mount Le Conte is open from mid-March to late-November for guests willing to hike the steep trail to the summit.*

beating wings struck the soft earth creating valleys. When he lifted his wings, they created the mountains which would be the Cherokees' home on earth.

The Appalachians are among the oldest mountain ranges in North America. A billion years ago, 3.6 billion years after the earth formed, the rocks of the Appalachian chain and those in the park were metamorphosed and partially melted in the first mountain-building phase. Their long history attests to the ever-occurring massive upheavals in the earth's crust.

Between 600 and 800 million years ago, sand, clay, and other sediment that were to become the present bedrock in the park were carried down from these early billion-year-old mountains and deposited into an ancient ocean, called Iapetus. More and more sediment emptied into the new ocean basin until the tremendous pressure of 30,000 feet of sediment slowly combined with the chemical action of water to cement the deep ocean sediment into rocks. This was the formation of the *Ocoee* series of rocks that underlay much of the Smoky Mountains.

Different kinds of rocks affect the shapes and forms of valleys and mountains, that is, the topography of the park. Rocks of the Anakeesta Formation are named for Anakeesta Ridge and are metamorphosed fine silt and mud or shales that originated in the Iapetus sea. These rocks have very thin layers and easily fall apart. Large masses of rock break off to form landslides that make very steep slopes and pinnacles such as those found at the Chimneys.

***T*he popular Laurel Falls trail** *starts with a walk through a pine-oak forest and advances into a cove hardwood forest of maples, tuliptrees, and dogwoods. Near the rocky sandstone outcrops at the falls, rock tripe covers the face of the rocks. This one-half-inch-tall lichen secretes an acid that helps break down rocks into soil. Laurel Falls is fed from a spring deep in Cove Mountain. The water from Laurel Branch flows into Little River and eventually arrives in the Gulf of Mexico. Most visitors are unaware of the virgin hardwood forest one-half mile beyond the falls.*

Thick sandstone beds comprise the Thunderhead Formation. Attractive Laurel Falls, near the Sugarlands Visitor Center, flows over this erosion-resistant sandstone. Boulder fields consist of large sandstone boulders, from 1 to 30 feet in diameter. These boulders accumulated during the constant freezing and thawing of the last ice age and are located along the bases of steep slopes. Some of the largest boulder deposits in eastern North America occur in the park. Good examples may be seen in the Greenbrier vicinity along the hiking trail to Ramsay Cascades Falls and the Newfound Gap Road near the Chimney Tops.

The Appalachians and Plate Tectonics

The Smoky Mountains are part of the ancient Appalachian mountain chain that runs southwest to northeast, a distance of about 2,000 miles, from central Alabama to Newfoundland. Clingmans Dome, the highest peak in the park, is 6,643 feet in elevation. This is just 41 feet lower than Mt. Mitchell, the highest mountain in eastern North America, located about 70 miles east.

To understand how these mountains came about we must understand the long and complex geologic history of eastern North America. Today, geologists believe that the earth's surface or *crust* is made of gigantic plates that slowly move around, floating on the hot liquid or melted rocks of the earth's interior. When plates collide, earthquakes, volcanoes, and mountain building occur.

The Smoky Mountains were created when Africa and North America were pushed against each other. They last separated about 200 million years ago. Rocks that were once at least 50,000 feet below the earth's surface were uplifted, folded, and fractured. It is estimated that at one time the Smoky Mountains were as high as 20,000 feet, similar to today's Himalayas.

Our imagination must stretch to realize the magnitude of geological activity in the park. In Cades Cove, for example, geologists know that younger rocks occur in the valley floor below older rocks on the mountainsides surrounding the cove. Great *tectonic* or mountain-building forces pushed the older rocks up and over the younger ones. Erosion of the older rocks has exposed this unusual geologic feature. Now that the younger bedrock is exposed, visitors in Cades Cove can actually stand on the youngest rocks of the park and look up over 3,000 feet at rocks some 300 million years older. A dozen streams and branches drain the valley into Abrams Creek which flows west of the cove where it enters Chilhowee Lake, the lowest elevation of the park.

WATER AND EROSION

Since the 1830s, scientists have suggested that at least four times in the last 1.5 million years, much of the northern hemisphere was submerged, with glaciers receding and advancing. During this time,

MARK E. GIBSON

Erosion by water brought these rocks tumbling down to become part of the Oconaluftee River. The angular boulders, over eons of time, have been rounded and smoothed by water action to help create a scene that suggests timeless serenity. Fast-moving currents and slippery rocks create dangerous situations, and care should be taken when wading.

Forces **pushed** the older **rocks** up and **over** the **younger** ones.

ADAM JONES

American mountain ash with its red berries complements the view from Clingmans Dome. Research has shown that scenic views such as these are becoming rarer in the park. Airborne pollutants emitted mostly outside the park are degrading resources and visitor enjoyment. Since 1948 the average visibility in the southern Appalachians has decreased 80 percent in the summer. Annual average visibility is 22 miles, compared to natural conditions of 93 miles.

NYE SIMMONS

The dark brown siltstone and slate of the *Anakeesta formation contain the mineral pyrite or iron sulfide. When this rock is disturbed and exposed to air and water, it creates sulfuric acid. In one unfortunate road-building incident in 1963, road fill material of Anakeesta stone was placed in Beech Flats Prong. The acid from the rock killed brook trout for about three miles along the stream.*

ice may have covered as much as a third of the earth's surface. Now, only about a tenth remains under ice. Although glaciers never made it this far south, they had a profound effect on climate in the park.

The geological story of landscape erosion continues, and at times these changes can be very dramatic. On September 1, 1951, a cloudburst on Mount Le Conte sent huge trees, rocks, and mud crashing down the mountain leaving vast scars in their wake. These scars are visible today along the Newfound Gap Road. Alum Cave Creek became a raging flood during this cloudburst. In June of 1993 another cloudburst of localized intensity created a flash flood 20 feet high that eroded the trail and the banks along Alum Cave Creek down to bedrock. In October 1995 Hurricane Opal damaged the Alum Cave trail so badly that it had to be closed for substantial repairs.

Water played a major role in sculpting the land. Today, at high-elevation vistas, the parallel drainages, where rock strata are eroded in parallel bands, are very evident. These and other streams create beautiful waterfalls which remind us of the mighty force of water at work in this environment.

SUGGESTED READING

Houk, Rose. *A Natural History Guide: Great Smoky Mountains National Park*. New York: Houghton Mifflin Company, 1993.

Mooney, James. *History, Myths, and Sacred Formulas of the Cherokees*. Asheville, NC: Historical Images, 1989 (Reprint 1891).

Moore, Harry. *A Roadside Geology of the Great Smoky Mountains National Park*. Knoxville: The University of Tennessee Press, 1988.

Walker, Stephen. *Great Smoky Mountains: The Splendor of the Southern Appalachians*. Charlottesville, VA: Elan Publishing, 1991.

***R**oadways in the park lead past* places of interesting history. Six hundred million years ago these rocks were created in an ocean basin when only soft-shelled primitive life existed. Today rhododendrons and eastern hemlocks adorn the road cut. Newfound Gap Road is also known as U.S. Highway 441 and is the park's only over-the-mountain road.

MARY ANN KRESSIG

CONNIE TOOPS

***A**nakeesta rock is shaly, breakable,* and dangerous to climb. Outcrops at Newfound Gap are inclined to the southeast, reflecting ancient mountain-building forces in the Smokies.

GEORGE HUMPHRIES

***M**oss-covered* sandstone boulders are usually slippery, unstable, and not good for crossing. Hikers have been stranded by fast rising streams, and every eventuality should be taken into consideration when hiking.

The Place of a Thousand Drips is at the end of the Roaring Fork Motor Nature Trail. This waterfall appears to be part of a garden landscape designed to cascade gently over the rocks. In reality it is slowly cutting away at bedrock and will probably create a small cove. Liverworts, mosses, and ferns make their home in this cool, moist setting.

NYE SIMMONS

CLINT FARLINGER

Meigs Falls beside Little River Road is named after Colonel Return Jonathan Meigs, United States Agent to the Cherokees from 1801 to 1823. Meigs surveyed one of the Indian treaty lines in what is now the park. The falls can only be observed from a vehicle pullout since no trails lead to it.

Sandstone boulders make Big Creek a good place for trout fishing. Crestmont, a Civilian Conservation Camp, was formerly on the site of the campground. Logging occurred here in the early 1900s. Largely undiscovered except by fishermen and wildflower enthusiasts, Big Creek is one of the quieter spots in the park.

PAT & CHUCK BLACKLEY

Relentless Water — in All Seasons

FRANK S. BALTHIS

The original wooden bridge constructed by the Little River Lumber Company for their logging railroad was later utilized by the park for its Little River Road. In February 1966, a devastating flood damaged the road and bridge. The bridge was repaired and the road was reopened in April 1966. The stone work was added in 1972-73. Nearby, The Sinks is a popular swimming hole but very dangerous with strong undercurrents and a rocky bottom.

*Mention Great Smoky
     Mountains National Park,
          and the first animal
     that comes to mind
          is the black bear.*

The Living Forest

In this majestic forest, over 130 species of trees cover the mountains with five distinctive forest types—spruce-fir, northern hardwood, cove hardwood, hemlock, and pine and oak. Trees set unofficial boundaries for their respective habitats which helps us to identify forest communities and the life that is within.

Boreal forests are present throughout the northern latitudes of the earth. Millions of years ago remnants of this coniferous forest were "pushed" southward to the southern Appalachians. Only a few other places in the southeastern United States host spruce-fir forests. All are in the southern Appalachians, and the spruce-fir forest in the park represents 74 percent of the entire remaining population. The spruce-fir forest defines the high-elevation habitat found along the spine of the mountains in the park. The nearest other forests of this type are found in Canada.

The northern hardwood forest is the highest-elevation broad-leaved forest in the East, occurring from about 4,000 to 5,800 feet. The prominent trees are the American beech, yellow birch, yellow buckeye, basswood, and striped maple. Ferns, coneflowers, skunk goldenrods, Rugel's ragworts, and spring beauties are found on the forest floor. Bear, deer, turkey, grouse, and red squirrel may be seen and heard in this area.

Cove hardwood forests are located in mountain coves which provide shelter from threatening high winds. The park's larger trees are found here in the deeper, richer soil and include beech, yellow buckeye, birch, black cherry, tuliptree or

*E*tched against the skyline is the unmistakable straight and tall tuliptree or yellow-poplar. The tuliptrees
in a young, mixed deciduous forest will reclaim the disturbed site quickly. Often found in pure stands, they prefer
moist soils in coves. In autumn they display a yellow leaf, and in spring a yellow and orange showy flower from
one and a half to two inches in size. These trees were favored by early settlers for building various farm structures.

Moss-covered eastern hemlock are found along many *trails. A champion tree from the park with a circumference of 16 feet 10 inches is listed in the* National Register of Big Trees*. Hemlocks are evergreens and have flat needles, with roughly grooved bark in older trees. An egg-shaped cone three-quarters-inch long can be used to identify the tree. The preferred habitat is moist slopes and ravines. One eastern hemlock found in an old-growth forest was 504 years old. It, and others, may be threatened by the introduced hemlock woolly adelgid.*

before creation of the park, and the influence of loggers can easily be spotted in the cove hardwoods which were eagerly sought by lumber companies.

The eastern hemlock forests, more common on the northern slopes with cooler temperatures, are found in wet, protected ravines and drainages up to an altitude of 4,500 feet. Along streams in this forest, which provide deep pools of water, muskrat, beaver, otter, and brook trout live.

The pine and oak forest is located on the dry, exposed, rocky southwest ridges, with pitch, short-leaf, Virginia, and table mountain pines in abundance. Several species of oak and red maple are part of this forest. A recently approved fire management plan provides direction and guidelines for the reintroduction of fire into this forest community.

Fire is important to the ecosystem. Table mountain pine requires fire to provide an open sunny condition and a mineral seedbed for reproduction. Fire also slows the takeover of pine lands by oaks. Pure stands of pines are needed for

yellow-poplar, sugar maple, hemlock, hickory, and magnolia. The tuliptree, related to the magnolia, has had a continuous lineage here for more than 50 million years. Cool, fast-flowing streams are found in these coves, and they host ferns, mosses, and a variety of flowers. Rosebay rhododendron thickets are usually found, along with mayapple, hydrangea, redbud, serviceberry, dogwood, and trillium. Red and gray fox roam here in search of food.

Evidence of plant succession can be found where settlers once lived and farmed. The tuliptree or yellow-poplar, a valuable hardwood tree, is the most noticeable and successful on disturbed sites. The Smoky Mountains were heavily logged

The tradition in the Great Smoky Mountains is to *hike to Gregory Bald in late June, or early July, to see the flame azaleas at their most gorgeous. At lower elevations, the flowering period begins in late April.*

There are 800 miles of hiking trails in the park, and all are as inviting as this one along Indian Camp Creek. The Maddron Bald Trail travels past Albright Grove to link with the Appalachian Trail at Inadu Knob. Inadu *is the* Cherokee name for "snake," and early settlers followed their example by naming the adjacent mountain Snake Den Ridge.

the endangered red-cockaded woodpecker whose habitat is found only in the Southeast. Years of suppressing natural fires upset the ecosystem balance, but the prescribed burn program that started in 1996 will help restore natural conditions.

Balds

Places in high elevations without forest cover are called balds. A Cherokee legend says the Great Spirit was pleased with the people for slaying a monster and willed that the highest mountains should be bare so enemies could always be seen.

Such areas are called heath balds if the shrubs—rhododendron, mountain-laurel, etc.—covering them are from the heath family. Heath is a corruption of the Scottish word heather, and the

name may have been used by early immigrants although no true heather grows here.

Grassy balds, those with grass and sedges, were favored by the early settlers for grazing livestock in pre-park days. There are about 20 grassy balds in the park, which may be overgrown in 30 to 70 years if natural succession of plants continues. Only two balds, Gregory and Parson, are "natural" as far as current historical evidence shows. Many are relics of European settlement.

To retain part of this historical landscape, the park manages Andrews and Gregory balds to keep them intact. Gregory Bald, above Cades Cove, was used for pasturage and is well known today for its beautiful flame azalea hybrids that bloom in late June.

BILL LEA

White-tailed deer began to decline in the 1930s due to hunting, disease, logging, and loss of habitat. The establishment of the park in 1934 helped restore them to their present successful numbers.

J & D RICHARDSON

Is this raccoon posed for fight or flight? These nocturnal mammals are found at all elevations of the park. They eat, among other things, wild grapes, salamanders, fish, and pokeberries.

WILDLIFE IN THE SMOKIES

Mention Great Smoky Mountains National Park, and the first animal that comes to mind is the black bear. The park is haven for 1,500 to 2,000 bears. Bears may occasionally be seen in daylight hours even though they are more active at night. They have a remarkable sense of smell and forage throughout the park for the berries, acorns, grasses, insects, and animals that make up their natural diet.

If bears are fed human food, they lose their wildness and begin to seek food along roadsides and at picnic areas and homesites, making them vulnerable to being hit by vehicles or killed by poachers. A major interpretive effort by the park encourages visitors not to feed bears or to leave food and garbage out because such acts may lead to the bears' untimely death.

A great diversity of birds find their niche within the park's five major forest types. The spruce-fir forest is the southernmost breeding range of the black-capped chickadee and golden-crowned kinglet. A mix of birds may be discovered at the altitude where the northern and cove hardwood forests merge. A good place to look for birds that require open areas, such as hawks and wild turkey, is the open fields of Cades Cove and Cataloochee. To date, 241 species of birds have been recorded in the park, of which 58 are permanent residents. An additional 118 species breed in the park. Christmas bird counts, conducted since 1935—one year after establishment of the park—record around 65 species.

NEOTROPICAL MIGRANTS

Worldwide about 340 species of birds are classified as neotropical migrants. There is concern about the declining population of neotropical migratory birds through loss of natural habitat and stopovers in both the tropics and the United States. The park's half-million acres is the largest contiguous forested habitat in the East and contains one of the highest diversities of breeding neotropical migratory birds.

Some neotropical migrants that nest in the park include the orchard oriole, scarlet and summer tanagers, yellow-breasted chat, Kentucky warbler, ovenbird, American redstart, white-eyed vireo, and broad-winged hawk. In an amazing feat of navigation and endurance each April, many migrants that winter in northern South America cross the more-than-600-mile Gulf of Mexico, and eventually arrive in the park. The ruby-throated hummingbird, which winters in Mexico and Central America, is the smallest bird in the park, laying two eggs each about the size of a pea.

AQUATIC SPECIES

Fog and rain, the lifeblood of the mountains, contribute to life within the park. At high elevations over 80 inches of precipitation are recorded, while the lower elevations record 54 inches. This precipitation provides 2,000 miles of clear unspoiled mountain streams that create peace and serenity in a fast-paced world—as well as some of the best fishing for rainbow and brown trout in the eastern United States. The park's only native trout, the genetically unique and protected southern Appalachian brook trout, lives in the headwaters and, if caught, must be returned to the stream. About 350 aquatic insects live in this habitat, providing food for the trout.

IRENE HINKE-SACILOTTO

The black-capped chickadee's breeding season is in late April or early May. It likes to nest in tree cavities created by other birds and will utilize dead yellow birch trees for nest sites. The black-capped is most easily distinguished from the Carolina chickadee by their different songs.

Even though the red fox, distinguishable by the white tip on its tail, is found throughout the park, it is not very common.

BILL LEA

The
Black Bears
here *are*
more *active*
at *night*.

One way to know nature is in balance is through observation of *indicator species* such as the salamander. Salamanders could not survive here if the water were not of good quality. Thankfully, they are plentiful. Thirty species of salamanders, in twelve different genera, give the Smoky Mountains the distinction of having the most diverse salamander population in the world. The Jordan's species has carved a special niche for itself. The red-cheeked form of this salamander is

These red-cheeked salamanders, a variation of Jordan's salamander, are found only in the high-elevation spruce-fir forests of the Great Smoky Mountains. Adults grow to be about six inches long.

HARRY ELLIS

restricted to the park, while the red-legged form is located south and outside of the park.

DIVERSITY OF PLANTS

An outstanding feature of the Smoky Mountains is its diversity of plants. Because of the climatic change from low to high elevation, one can experience the same forests and habitats as if traveling from the low-elevation towns of Cherokee or Gatlinburg to Canada.

Although glaciers did not reach the Smoky Mountains, they were a mile thick less than 500 miles to the north in Pennsylvania and west in Ohio. Because of their proximity, they had a great influence on climate in the park. The alternating cooling and warming cycles "pushed" or forced plants from the extent of their northern range to a new southern one.

When the ice age ended and the climate warmed, some plants and animals migrated up-slope, and became isolated from their kin going north. One of many such plants found in the park is wood sorrel, which is a common ground cover in spruce-fir forests. It is native to Canada as well, but has adapted to the southern mountaintops. Other flora and fauna which moved ahead of the advancing cold of the glaciers include the northern flying squirrel, twinflowers, mountain paper birch trees, and saw-whet owls.

CHAMPION TREES

Although water is often considered the major player in the mountains, equal billing should perhaps be given to trees. The park has 17 national champion trees—identified as the largest specimen of their species—growing in America. Such champion trees include sourwood, yellow buck-

eye, eastern hemlock, red maple, Allegheny serviceberry, and devil's walkingstick.

By mid-September the first faint color appears in the highest elevations when yellow birch, American beech, mountain maple, and pin cherry begin their annual display. The spectacular colors peak in October. During the last two weeks of October, sugar maple, scarlet oak, red maple, and hickory are in full glory.

Often overlooked because of the beautiful fall leaf display are the many roadside and meadow flowers with such interesting names as mountain mist, New York ironweed, cardinal flower, bee-balm, Maryland golden aster, Canada goldenrod, and coneflower.

Whether it is the glorious wildflowers of spring, the spectacular color of autumn, the snow-bound solitude of winter, or the cool green of summer, there are mystery and beauty waiting to be discovered every day of the year. A complex and fragile world competes for survival here, but is often overlooked because of the mountains' showy beauty.

SUGGESTED READING

Alsop, Fred III. *Birds of the Smokies*. Gatlinburg: Great Smoky Mountains Natural History Association, 1991.

National Park Handbook #112. *Great Smoky Mountains*. Washington, D.C.: National Park Service, 1981.

Rennicke, Jeff. *Black Bear*. Gatlinburg: Great Smoky Mountains Natural History Association, 1991.

Toops, Connie. *Great Smoky Mountains*. Stillwater, MN: Voyageurs Press, 1992.

White, Peter. *Wildflowers of the Smokies*. Gatlinburg: Great Smoky Mountains Natural History Association, 1996.

Flowering dogwood has beautiful yellow flowers and white bracts in the spring, with red fruit in the autumn that attracts birds and squirrels. The eastern redbud has pink flowers and blooms before the leaves appear.

LARRY ULRICH

This autumn scene with its strong, vibrant colors may be experienced by hiking the Thomas Divide Trail, built by the Civilian Conservation Corps. It is one of the longest individual trails in the park. The Great Smoky Mountains is part of the larger Blue Ridge province which, in turn, is a part of the Appalachian Highlands. Hernando De Soto, an explorer, named the Appalachian Mountains after a tribe of Florida Gulf Coast Indians, the Apalachee.

ADAM JONES

Overleaf: Early morning views of ridges and valleys shrouded by fog inspire peace and serenity. Photo by George Humphries.

Along the Oconaluftee River asters gracefully overlook a field of sedges.

LARRY ULRICH

The creamy-white flowers of Dutchman's breeches will be easy to name if one thinks of trousers hanging from a clothesline to dry.

GEORGE HUMPHRIES

GENE COX

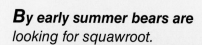

PAT TOOPS

Tennessee's state flower, the crested dwarf iris, blooms throughout the lower elevations in April and May.

The distinctive moccasin shape of the yellow lady's slipper orchid assists in identification.

The wild geranium is one of the park's early bloomers.

By early summer bears are looking for squawroot.

GEORGE HUMPHRIES

BILL LEA

The Smokies in Bloom

J & D RICHARDSON

GEORGE HUMPHRIES

Wake robin trillium and fringed phacelia, which bloom in early spring in mid to high elevations, grace many trails in the park.

GEORGE HUMPHRIES

Pollinated by flies, this easily recognizable jack-in-the-pulpit has a mass of brilliant red berries when it goes to seed in late summer. A less imaginative name is Indian turnip.

CONNIE TOOPS

The pods of mature pale jewelweed explode when touched, giving rise to the more common name—touch-me-not.

LARRY ULRICH

beauty
waiting *to*
be discovered

The small white flowers of wild stonecrop are strikingly beautiful against the deep green of its succulent leaves. The habitat is moist, moss-covered rocks, trees, and stream banks. People of southern Appalachia say that if stonecrop grows well near the home, good times will follow.

Gray squirrels are usually *found in the lower elevations of the park in deciduous forests where they enjoy fruits of the flowering dogwood.*

BILL LEA

The common gray treefrog (which *may be gray, brown, green, or pearl-gray) forages aloft in small trees and shrubs near water.*

ADAM JONES

The river otter, *gone from the region by the time the park was established in 1934, was successfully reintroduced in 1994 with a release of 100. These curious animals feed mostly on crayfish, suckers, and stonerollers.*

BILL LEA

The hemlock varnish shelf fungus *is found on coniferous wood, especially hemlock. It grows from May through November, and each ring of this colorful fungus represents one year's development. These are probably several years old. The underside has a pleasantly brilliant burnt-orange color.*

MARY ANN KRESSIG

The park is home for 1,500 to 2,000 black bears, one of the highest population densities in the world for this animal. The large acreage of the park provides the habitat diversity and range they need. They are agile climbers and like to sleep and seek food in trees. Life begins in the winter. While the sow is deep in hibernation, from one to five cubs are born. When born they weigh less than half a pound, but will be ready to leave the den by early April. Bears will eat meat but plants make up over three-fourths of their diet.

IRENE HINKE-SACILOTTO

***T**he white-eyed vireo prefers thickets and usually* lays four white eggs, brown-dotted, in a nest only a few feet off the ground. The opportunistic brown-headed cowbird will use the vireo's nest for its own eggs, which are about the same color.

Winged Creatures

***H**earing the trilling of an eastern screech-owl in the evening is one of the great experiences of nature. This young owl will grow to a length of about ten inches. Found throughout the park, screech-owls can be identified by their yellow eyes, small size, and large sharp claws for capturing their prey.*

IRENE HINKE-SACILOTTO

STEPHEN J. KRASEMANN

***W**ild turkeys are found most often at Cades Cove* and Cataloochee, where there is open woodland. Nesting on the ground, the females lay from 10 to 15 buff eggs with black and brown spots. The male can sometimes be 48 inches tall— about the height of an eight-year-old child. With improved wildlife management they have increased in numbers in the eastern United States.

Dark-eyed juncos *migrate in elevation within the park, going to the higher coniferous forest in summer and coming down the mountain to winter in fields and roadside thickets. The mother lays three to five pale green, brown-spotted eggs in a cuplike nest.*

IRENE HINKE-SACILOTTO

The male ruby-throated hummingbird is *identified by a brilliant red gorget on its throat. This female has hatched her young from two white pea-sized eggs. Ruby-throated hummingbirds arrive in the park around the end of April. Red flowers like bee balm and thistle attract them. Hummingbirds are the park's smallest birds, and their needlelike bills are used for sipping nectar from flowers.*

The caterpillar of the Eastern tiger *swallowtail butterfly feeds on a variety of trees and shrubs. In a common behavior, called puddling, the adult butterflies group in large numbers around moist places on the ground.*

GEORGE HUMPHRIES

IRENE HINKE-SACILOTTO

-31-

"The Painted Rock on the French Broad River;
thence along the highest ridge
of said mountain to the place
where it is called
the Great Iron or Smoky Mountains..."

Those Who Came Before...

The Alfred Reagan tub mill on the Roaring Fork Motor Nature Trail is still operable. About two dozen families lived along the creek and supported a store, church, school, and a few tub mills to grind cornmeal or chicken feed.

SALVATORE VASAPOLLI

Native Americans were the first to explore the Smoky Mountains. Sometime around the year 1000 the Cherokees, of Iroquoian stock, migrated to the mountains and claimed the land. The first European to encounter them was probably De Soto in 1540. They occupied all of Kentucky and portions of seven other states, with a population of perhaps 22,000. Much of this land was lost through treaties, and by 1835 they controlled only a few million acres.

In 1827 the Cherokees established a governmental system and created their own Constitution in eastern Tennessee, with Chota as the capital of the Overhill Towns. They were organized into seven clans, had a matriarchal society and lived in log houses in the foothills of the present-day park. By using an alphabet, or syllabary, developed by one of their members, Sequoyah, they published their own newspaper and books. Recognition came to Sequoyah on the far side of the continent, with the western redwood trees and a national park carrying his name, spelled Sequoia.

In 1838 President Martin Van Buren ordered the removal of the Cherokees to the Oklahoma territory. About 1,000 Cherokees refused to move and remained in Georgia, North Carolina, Alabama, and Tennessee. Big Cove on the eastern boundary of the park was the last stronghold of the Cherokees in their fight to remain. Later, those residing in western North Carolina became known as the Eastern Band of Cherokees and were recognized by both the federal and state governments.

When settlers came to places such as Cades Cove, they found deer and other wildlife in abundance. Wildlife provided food, clothing, and hides for use around the farm.

TOM ALGIRE

Their descendants live on the present day Cherokee Indian Reservation adjacent to the park.

PIONEER SETTLEMENT

After the American Revolution, a poor nation paid its soldiers with its greatest natural asset—land. Soldiers, who often could not afford land, or were not even allowed to own land in their ancestral homelands, were very pleased to be paid in this method, believing it meant wealth. These soldier/settlers and their families began to push westward with their few possessions, trading and selling land to improve their lot. Many went to the fertile bottomlands and mountains of the Appalachians.

Settlement had increased enough by 1789 that the federal government formed the "Territory South of the River Ohio." In defining the boundary, which extended to "the Painted Rock on the French Broad River; thence along the highest ridge of said mountain to the place where it is called the Great Iron or Smoky Mountains...," we find the first official use of the name Smoky.

In North Carolina Cataloochee was part of a Revolutionary War grant, and by 1814 the first claim had been made. Cataloochee was known by the Cherokees as *Ga-da-lu-tsi*—"high mountain peaks standing up in a row surrounding the valley." By the 1900s settlers had constructed nearly 200 buildings in the Cataloochee valley. Other early nineteenth-century settlements included Gatlinburg and Cades Cove in Tennessee. Cades Cove prospered, and by 1850 it had 137 households, with a population of 685.

Although self-sufficient, members of these communities shopped or "traded" at nearby towns. All the amenities that others of their generation had, including doctors, newspapers, schools,

This meathouse was moved from the Little Cataloochee *valley to the Mountain Farm Museum in the 1950s. Constructed of logs with half-dovetail notches, it was one of the most important buildings on the family farm. Meat, usually pork, was butchered in the fall, salted, cured, and stored here.*

IMPACT OF LOGGING

Logging, too, had a dramatic impact on the region. By the late 1800s practically all the forests of the northeast United States had been harvested. The steam-powered circular saw had modernized the lumber industry, contributing to the rapid rate at which trees could be harvested. Cut timber could be taken to the sawmill, sawed into lumber, and with the advent of the railroad easily shipped to markets.

The nation was growing rapidly, and wood was used for almost everything. Entire wood homes, for example, could be ordered from mail-order catalogs. Lumbermen were looking everywhere for forests to satisfy this need. They found a solution in the southern mountains, with their

regular mail service, religious services, and community social activities, were available to them. Except for the clearing of land for crops, the mountains were almost unchanged from the way the early settlers found them in Revolutionary War days. However, although the land was relatively untouched, wolves, bison, and elk were eradicated in the region within 100 years through hunting and trapping.

The logging era brought industrialization to *the mountains on a scale they had never known before. Railroads built to haul away the fallen logs defied ordinary limits of construction. This swinging bridge transported logs across the water at Meigs Creek and Little River.*

The white basswood tree normally grows to a height of 60 to 125 feet, but the park record is 135 feet. The wood is white, soft, and clear—and used in cabinetwork. In May the creamy flowers have an almost tropical aroma. Bees are attracted to the nectar which makes good honey. Nut-like seeds fall to the ground in autumn to be stored and eaten by mice and chipmunks. In winter ruffed grouse and deer feed on the edible buds.

large virgin hardwood tracts and cheap prices.

Hazel Creek, a lumber town, was settled in the 1830s. Although it was sparsely populated throughout much of the nineteenth century, most families were farmers. Industrialization began at the turn of the century, with the beginning of copper mining in the nearby Sugar Fork drainage. With the arrival of the railroad to Hazel Creek in 1907 and the building of a large sawmill operation at the community of Proctor, logging by the W. M. Ritter Lumber Company began in earnest in the Hazel Creek watershed. It was one of the largest logging operations in the Great Smoky Mountains and extended to the highest elevations in the mountains. By the time the operation closed in 1928,

Hazel Creek had been home to a thousand people and more than 200 million board feet of timber had been cut.

Once started, logging in the Smoky Mountains proceeded with a vengeance. Railroads were built to the top of the mountains. Sawmills were quickly installed, and towns sprang up in what would later become the park. At one time 2,000 people lived at the sawmill town of Smokemont where a park campground is now located.

For the next 40 years, the mountains reverberated with the buzz and whine of sawmills. Immense trees were cut, with many logs measuring six feet in diameter. Almost four-fifths of the future park was logged. Fortunately, at least 100,000 acres

When the American chestnut tree declined in old-growth forests, the canopy opened. Increased availability of sunlight and minerals fostered the growth of oaks and other species.

FRANK S. BALTHIS

creation of the National Park Service in 1916.

Horace Kephart, in his 1913 book *Our Southern Highlanders*, advocated the establishment of a national park in the Smoky Mountains. The successful movement for a Great Smoky Mountains National Park was officially started by Mr. and Mrs. Willis P. Davis of Knoxville, Tennessee, in 1923. Groups in North Carolina joined this effort, and by 1934 the park was established.

Perhaps no one group contributed more to the development of facilities and long-lasting enjoyment of the park than the young men of the Civilian Conservation Corps. Created in May of 1933, during the Depression, the CCC eventually had 22 permanent and temporary camps scattered throughout the park. These men built almost all of the hiking trails, magnificent stone highway bridges, roads, and fire towers in the national park. Mt. Cammerer, the only stone tower in the Smoky Mountains, which has been restored by the park's Friends group, was part of this work.

Threats to the Park

In 1956 it was discovered that the spruce-fir boreal forest in the southern Appalachians was being threatened by a small, aphid-like insect from Europe, the balsam woolly adelgid. The adelgid feeds on the sap of the Fraser firs causing them to die, thus devastating entire stands. Alarmingly, these trees also host a very rare spruce-fir moss spider, which is threatened due to loss of habitat, along with several nationally rare mosses. In this same habitat is Rugel's ragwort, which is not known to exist anywhere but in the high Smoky Mountains. The question of how these species will survive in a devastated forest remains to be answered.

Nationwide, air quality is an important issue and in the Great Smoky Mountains, as elsewhere, ground-level ozone pollution threatens human health and vegetation. Nitrogen and sulfur depositions acidify soils and streams, which can harm trees and fish. Fossil-fuel-fired power plants, industrial processes, and motor vehicles are the primary sources of these pollutants. Thirty or more species of plants in the park show visible leaf damage from ozone injury.

of uncut forest remain, making it one of the last large virgin forests in the East.

Entire mountainsides were cut without regard for the environment. Once the mountainsides were cleared, there was nothing to prevent serious erosion. Resinous brush from harvested species often caught fire at high elevations, where fire is extremely infrequent naturally, and this contributed to the washing away of topsoil.

A Special Place is Protected

This devastation was not entirely ignored. There were visionaries who saw the value and diversity of this mountain land and wanted to protect it. One of the earliest, Dr. Chase P. Ambler of Asheville, North Carolina, organized and directed an intensive campaign from 1889 to 1905 for a national park in the southern Appalachians. This and other early attempts throughout the United States eventually culminated in the

High above Cades Cove on Gregory Bald, the National Park Service uses fire in controlled burns as a management tool to help preserve the balds. Some species that benefit from fire, a natural process, are the endangered red-cockaded woodpecker, black oak, Table Mountain pine, golden seal, dwarf larkspur, and Indian grass. Fire opens the sealed cones of Table Mountain pine, dispersing seeds over fire-cleared ground—and the red-cockaded woodpecker will nest only in mature pine trees that are clear of underbrush.

MICHAEL COLLIER

The scenic quality for which the park was protected has changed dramatically. Within the last 50 years, average annual visibility has been reduced from 93 miles to 22 miles. Air quality monitoring and research stations have been established in the park, and an active program is being pursued to improve air quality in the region.

There are numerous other threats to the park lands, significant not only to the environment but also to the economy of the region. Although these threats may be similar to those in other parks, it is the blend of large and small, special species, unique habitats, and the interdependence of them all which make the Smoky Mountains a very special place.

SUGGESTED READING

Campbell, Carlos. *Birth of a National Park*. Knoxville: The University of Tennessee Press, 1984.

Frome, Michael. *Strangers in High Places*. Knoxville: The University of Tennessee Press, 1980.

National Park Handbook #125. *At Home in the Smokies*. Washington, D.C.: National Park Service, 1984.

Shields, A. Randolph. *The Cades Cove Story*. Gatlinburg: Great Smoky Mountains Natural History Association, 1981.

Trout, Ed. *Historic Buildings of the Smokies*. Gatlinburg: Great Smoky Mountains Natural History Association, 1995.

Entire mountainsides were *cut* without *regard* for the environment.

ADAM JONES

These white, stark, Fraser firs stand like gravestones of death in an otherwise beautiful scene of fog in timeless space —a contrast of destruction and peaceful harmony in the high coniferous forest of the southern Appalachians. An introduced insect, the balsam woolly adelgid, may destroy the last of the Fraser fir forests in the park.

Cades Cove

Demonstrations of pioneer activities are presented as special programs to help interpret the cultural history of the park. The Maryville Index announced the arrival of a blacksmith in 1878 saying his ironworking skills "would supply a long needed want."

NYE SIMMONS

CONNIE TOOPS

Ballads were sung in earlier times in Cades Cove, with religion having a great influence on music. After the Civil War harp singing of hymns, unaccompanied by music, was endorsed by the churches which did not support other songs. Bluegrass music of more recent heritage started in the 1930s.

Dan Lawson, one of the more prosperous people in the community, paid for the construction of the Methodist Church in 1880. He also built his home, circa 1856, with a brick chimney, unusual for the time and place. This barn and other farm buildings are all representative of nineteenth-century rural architecture in Cades Cove.

JOHN ELK III

JOHN ELK III

Organized in 1827 the original Primitive Baptist Church was built of logs and served the community until the present one was built in 1887. The nearby Missionary Baptist Church was built in 1902. The two churches split in 1839 because some of the members supported missionary work and having Sunday schools, both national issues among Baptists. The division continues, with Primitive and Missionary Baptist churches divided on the interpretation of the Scriptures.

"Hamp" Tipton settled in Cades Cove a few years after the Civil War and built the Tipton-Oliver home. Nearby, this double pen corn crib is larger than average. The two-story cantilever barn with two storage pens on the ground level was reconstructed in 1968, replacing the original that stood on the site. The foundation is of loose fieldstone. The storage pens are hand-hewn saddle-notched logs while the upper portion is made of sawn lumber.

NYE SIMMONS

Mountain Farm Museum and Cherokee

Atlas and Ball canning jars are just memories to most of us. Preserving food in these containers was a major summer task.

Woodworking was a useful skill on the farm. This volunteer is carving a replica spoon to be used in the park's cultural history program.

Mingus Mill had a wholesale and retail business. Many mills used waterwheels for power, but this mill has an 1890s water-powered turbine still used for grinding cornmeal.

Cornbread, one of the greatest mountain dishes, is made from cornmeal, salt, soda, baking powder, buttermilk, and perhaps an egg. Mix all this together, and bake at 500 °F in an iron skillet in which a tad of grease has been heated.

The Enloe-Floyd barn at the Mountain Farm Museum is the only building original to the site. It was built between the mid- to late-1800s by the Enloe family. The barn is huge, 50 by 60 feet, and is of a shotgun design with an even number of stalls along both sides of the hallway.

ADAM JONES

the **wood** *carving* of **Sequoyah** stands guard

This **wood carving of Sequoyah, who founded the Cherokee** *Syllabary, stands guard over the Museum of the Cherokee Indian in Cherokee, North Carolina. The story of the Cherokee Indian is a fascinating one. Theirs is a culture of great leadership, tragedy, and perseverance. Few realize these ancient people lived in log cabins, tilled their farms, and had their own newspaper and written language. The Cherokee survived the tragic Trail of Tears march to Oklahoma in 1838-39 with around 800 receiving permission from the U.S. Government to stay in the vicinity of the park.*

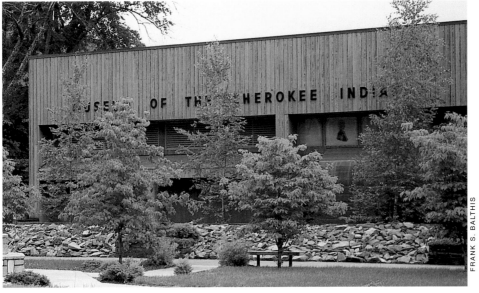

FRANK S. BALTHIS

ADAM JONES

Hikers leave the pavement at Newfound Gap to travel a portion of the 71 miles of the Appalachian Trail found in the park. In the 1930s, this section, and much of the entire 2,155-mile trail, was constructed by the Civilian Conservation Corps. The concept of having a route to preserve the crest of the Appalachian mountains and provide a secluded place to enjoy the wildlands was very innovative. The trail was finally completed in 1951.

These second-grade students are taking part in the Parks as Classroom program, studying the role Mingus Mill played in the community. The students tour the mill and learn how the forest community was both a supermarket and a drugstore to the early settlers. They make wooden toys just like children did at the turn of the century, and they compare early mountain settlements with their modern-day communities.

Rainbow and brown trout may be caught in over 700 miles of streams—some of the best flyfishing in the east. Brook trout, the park's only native trout species, are protected in 120 miles of streams closed to fishing.

Water's up! A familiar call to kayakers in the spring when rain has increased the volume of Little River making it suitable to kayak and test one's skill.

All About Great Smoky Mountains National Park

Great Smoky Mountains Natural History Association

The Great Smoky Mountains Natural History Association, founded by a group of National Park Service employees in 1953, is a non-profit organization which helps support the educational, research, and scientific activities of the park. The association doesn't just sell books—it publishes them as well. Numerous award-winning publications on the Smokies have been produced that enhance public enjoyment and understanding. A residential environmental education center managed by the association provides programs to schools, groups, and individuals. The association helps fund many major interpretive projects and programs such as wayside and museum exhibits, historic demonstrations and festivals, and the operation of the park library. Since its creation the GSMNHA has given over three million dollars in aid and services to the park.

CONTACT INFO:

Call the park at:
865-436-1200

Write to:
Great Smoky Mountains
National Park
107 Park Headquarters
Road
Gatlinburg, TN 37738

Visit the park's web site at:
www.nps.gov/grsm

For information on road conditions, call:
865-436-1200

Great Smoky Mountains Junior Ranger Program

The delicate
foamflower blooms

Becoming an official Great Smoky Mountains Junior Ranger is a fun way to learn and appreciate the many various plants and animals living within the park, as well as the exciting history of the park.

To become an official Junior Ranger and receive a certificate, badge or patch just pick up a booklet ($3) at any park visitor center and complete the activities. The activities include learning what a "Park Ranger" does, as well as games, lessons, hikes, and ranger-led walks or talks.

The park's Junior Ranger program hopes to instill in kids (5-12 years old) an appreciation of the natural and cultural resources of the park and motivate them to become good stewards.

416

73

321 73

73

321 Greenbrier

Greenbrier Pinnacle

Mount
Cammerer

TENNESSEE
NORTH
CAROLINA

40

CHEROKEE
NATIONAL
FOREST

Foothills Parkway

Roaring Fork Motor Nature Trail

Greenbrier
Cove

Ramsay Cascades Trail

Ramsay
Cascades

Mount Guyot

Big Creek

PISGAH
NATIONAL
FOREST

40

Cherokee
Orchard

Grotto Falls

Rainbow Falls

Rainbow Falls Trail

Porters
Flat

Porters Creek Trail

Mount Chapman

Mount Sequoyah

Appalachian Trail

BALSAM MOUNTAIN

Cataloochee

Little Pigeon River

Mount Le Conte

Chimney Tops

Alum Cave Trail

Charlies Bunion

HUGHES RIDGE

West Prong Little Pigeon River

SUGARLAND MOUNTAIN

RICHLAND MOUNTAIN

Oconaluftee River

Raven Fork

Straight Fork Road

Balsam Mountain Road

CATALOOCHEE DIVIDE

NATIONAL   PARK

Clingmans Dome Road

Clingmans Dome
6643ft
2025m

Andrews Bald

Thomas Ridge

Smokemont

Big Cove Road

Raven Fork

Blue Ridge

Parkway

Heintooga Ridge Road

19

NOLAND DIVIDE

Oconaluftee
Visitor Center

Mountain Farm Museum

CHEROKEE INDIAN RESERVATION

441

CHEROKEE

19

441

Deep Creek

Bryson City

74

Tuckasegee River

Tuckasegee River

441

ALARKA MOUNTAINS

28

FOREST

23

441

VICINITY MAP

40 Knoxville

40

321 411

TENNESSEE
Newport

Sevierville

321

Gatlinburg

321

Maryville

321

GREAT SMOKY   MOUNTAINS

NATIONAL PARK

40

129

Cherokee

74

NORTH CAROLINA

Millions are attracted to fall displays in the forests of eastern North America. Each of the five major characteristic forest types in the park are different, yet in fall they blend together into one common denominator—color. It is this vastness of forest down to the smallest wildflower which can impress and inspire us. Trees have a tremendous impact on wildlife. One large oak tree can produce tens of thousands of acorns for bear, deer and squirrel. One poor nut production season can mean hunger or starvation. In this ecosystem of interrelationships one can grasp the simple joy of living, discovery, sanctuary, excitement and challenge. It can be an enriching experience and it belongs to all of us.

Newfound Gap Road winds across the Grat Smoky Mountains during one of the most colorful seasons of the year. Watch for gorgeous fall wildflowers along roadside and open areas.

Great Smoky Mountains Today

Great Smoky Mountains is the most popular national park in the United States, with more than 9 million visitors annually. Two-thirds are repeat visitors. Many enjoy the annual Wildflower Pilgrimage and Mountain Life Festival, two of the many special events that interpret the cultural and natural resources of the park. Like many parks, however, Great Smoky Mountains is staggering from heavy visitation and deteriorating visitor services, and is stressed from numerous resource threats, of which visitors often are not aware.

The Smoky Mountains—crown jewels of the Appalachians—are a place of superlatives, with 16 peaks over 6,000 feet in elevation. The park is home to 1,489 species of flowering plants, including about 130 types of trees. Seventy mammals have been identified. There are 38 types of reptiles and 58 freshwater varieties of fish. Historians, architects, and those who just enjoy older buildings delight in the park's superb collection of log structures, some 75 in all. Thousands find inspiration and recreation on 800 miles of hiking trails.

The park is a haven for the wide-ranging black bear and neotropical migratory birds. It is large enough to inventory, monitor, and serve as a barometer for how well we are doing as a park and as a nation in preserving our precious resources. If we are to protect this and other ecosystems responsibly, the support of all visitors is needed.

LARRY ULRICH

Asters dominate this riverside fall scene.

KC Publications has been the leading publisher of colorful, interpretive books about National Park areas, public lands, Indian lands, and related subjects for over 40 years. We have 6 active series—over 125 titles—with Translation Packages in up to 8 languages for over half the areas we cover. Write, call, or visit our web site for our full-color catalog.

Our series are:

The Story Behind the Scenery® – Compelling stories of over 65 National Park areas and similar Public Land areas. Some with Translation Packages.

in pictures...The Continuing Story® – A companion, pictorially oriented, series on America's National Parks. All titles have Translation Packages.

For Young Adventurers™ – Dedicated to young seekers and keepers of all things wild and sacred. Explore America's Heritage from A to Z.

Voyage of Discovery® – Exploration of the expansion of the western United States.

Indian Culture and the Southwest – All about Native Americans, past and present.

Calendars – For National Parks in dramatic full color and a companion Color Your Own series, with crayons.

To receive our full-color catalog featuring over 135 titles—Books, Calendars, Screen Scenes, Videos, Audio Tapes, and other related specialty products:

Call (800-626-9673), fax (702-433-3420), write to the address below, Or visit our web site at www.kcpublications.com

Published by KC Publications, 3245 E. Patrick Ln., Suite A, Las Vegas, NV 89120.

Inside back cover: Sugarland Valley captures the essence of the mountains. Photo by Adam Jones.

Back cover: The soft, misty appearance of Rainbow Falls belies the fact that it was formed by centuries of erosion. Photo by George Humphries.

Created, Designed, and Published in the U.S.A.
Printed by Tien Wah Press (Pte.) Ltd, Singapore
Pre-Press by United Graphic Pte. Ltd